Inner Mirror

ज़िंदगी के मायने, और उसीके आईने

Pratik Kolekar

BookLeaf Publishing
India | USA | UK

Made with ❤ on the BookLeaf Publishing Platform
www.bookleafpub.in
www.bookleafpub.com

Dedication

To my beloved wife and my best friend, Manali,
who has been my best supporter.
To my wonderful son, and the light of our lives, Ayan.
And to my dearest family, who have helped me
grow and prosper.

While my life is full of people, just like everyone else's, it's you who have been my greatest pillars, my motivators, and my unshakable source of faith. Whatever I do has been mostly built around you, with you, and for you. Your endless love, constant encouragement, and belief in me have been inspiring me to write every line, every verse, and use beautiful mirages of words to portray all kinds of life's experiences.

This book exists because you've always reminded me, and pushed me to keep writing. And I keep dreaming, and keep going back to this magical world of poetry because of you.

Let me also take some place on this page to dedicate it to all **my well-wishers and closest of friends**, who have acknowledged and appreciated my love for poetry.

Thank you!

Preface

This book is a collection born and bred over years. Written in quiet moments, in the middle of chaos, sitting in rickshaws, while travelling to different parts of the world, idling at work, musing at nights, and often in the in-between that we call life. This collection portrays the inner, humane side of us from different perspectives. Mirroring life's experiences, the love we feel, our fleeting emotions, and many other shades of the world we live in today. This collection is not bound by any style or form; instead, it wanders freely in various ways, much like life itself. And true to its diversity, some of the poems are in Hindi, others whisper in English.

The poems here have been drawn from personal journeys, others inspired by the things I've read, seen, by people I've met, everyday scenes, strangers, social media posts, and if nothing, then the silent echoes of my random, fuzzy thoughts. Some are long and lingering; others are miniatures, and some just two lines or dialogues that, on their own, hold a complete story.

I hope readers will truly live this book. Take a dive into it when you want to break free from the current world for something nostalgic, close to your heart. Read it, take a deep breath, pause, and revisit different times in your own life. Perhaps a poem will show you a reflection of your own feelings too, or some will bring to you something entirely new that you're yet to experience in life.

Ultimately, these poems are about life in its many forms. Whether it is the beauty, or the dark sides. Whether its ache, or happiness. Many sides, in life's unpredictable rhythm. I really hope you find something in this book that shows you an inner mirror, speaks to you in a unique way, and if even one line stays with you long after you've closed the book, then this journey will be totally worth it!

Acknowledgements

My heartfelt gratitude to my wife, whose unwavering encouragement led me to writing this book. Although she wished for a novel, this is definitely a hopeful start that she would love and appreciate. I hope I stand true to her steadfast belief in me that I feel has kept every page alive while I was writing. And someday, I hope I write a novel too. To my son, for inspiring me to embrace what I love, keeping the kid in me alive, and to chase life's adventures with open arms. And to my family, for always giving me the freedom to walk my own path.

I owe much to my life itself, to all its moments, emotions, people, and the experiences have found their way into these poems you hold today. To all the fellow writers and poets, whose words, sayings, and creations have inspired me to explore, experiment, and write in ways I always dreamt of. And to all those handful of people who have shown their love and support to my writing journey and poetic exploration. Thank you for being a part of it.

1. To be lost is to learn the way - An African Proverb

We are so scared of the unknown
Paths that have never been shown
Eyes busy in finding a Polaris
Seeking comfort, nothing amiss

So complacent taking the explored
That staff defining every chord
Those books full of knowledge
Guiding our lives at every stage

We have given up our passions
For all the easy attractions
We have forgotten the excitement
In the shackles of being content

Let that heart beat a little faster today
Let your nerves feel the rush of a foray
Let your mind unleash from its stay
Out there, to be lost is to learn the way

2. The doors

When one door closes, another one opens
Just keep trying, and the magic happens
You'll see days when the whole world darkens
But only after a storm, is light full of lessons

The opportunities always knock on your door
But you'll never ever know what's in store
Sail that rocky boat, then find your shore
When you've a voice, you'll learn to roar

Putting foot in certain doors can be daunting
But don't let the unknown be a haunting
Reach out to the light of your heart's chanting
You're always one step closer to your wanting

Don't slam a door, when you finally succeed
Lend your hand to those in need
When you know how it feels to bleed
You'll find solace when someone is freed

3. सपना तभी ख़त्म होता है...

कुछ मंज़िलों को पाना नामुमकिन हो
तो हम सपनों का सहारा लेते हैं
कितना अलग सा जहाँ होता है वह
कितना कुछ उसी में जी लेते हैं

शायद इन्हीं सपनों से हौसला मिल जाता है
फिर मंज़िल की ओर वापस चल देते हैं
आख़िर सपना तो तभी ख़त्म होता है
जब हम उसे देखना बंद कर देते हैं

4. Miniature | What are we?

What are we in this unending universe?
Just a little speck in the wild

Minds so big, we still can't immerse
In the thought that other worlds may collide

5. Miniature | किनारा

हवाओं का रूख मोड़ दो कुछ यूँ
मुझे छू जाए तो एहसास तुम्हारा हो
ना जाने ये लहरें तूफ़ानी सी क्यों हैं
मेरी कश्ती सवार ले, तुम वह किनारा हो

6. Miniature | I don't know

I don’t know
Whether it’s my heart being greedy
Or my mind is feeling needy

Like a pirate conquering seas for treasure
I seek validation, the unspoken pleasure
I don’t know

7. Guftagu | Baap

"Uski har zidd ko tyohar sa kyun manate ho?"

"Baap hu yaar, akhir haar hi jata hu."

8. Guftagu | Mehsus

"Itna pyaar toh kisi ne kisi se kiya nahi hoga."

"Mehsus karne wali baatein koi yun jatayega kaise?"

9. अजीब है

लोग तो कहते हैं सब लिखा हुआ है
क़िस्मत में लिखा बदला नहीं जाता
पर ये सब बस तभी मानते हैं
जब ख़ुशियों का कोई हिसाब नहीं होता

कभी ज़िंदगी में आँधी सी आए
और आँसुओं की जब कोई गिनती ना हो
दुआ माँगते हैं किस्मत पलट जाए
ये जो लिखा है उसे कोई बदल सा दो

अजीब है
हँसी हो या आंसू
हिसाब ही तो नसीब है

10. माँ तो हमेशा बस चिल्लाती थी

कुछ पानी गिरा था मेरे हाथों से
उसने घूरा मुझे बड़ी आँखों से
ना जाने इतनी सी चीज़ उसे क्यों सताती थी
माँ तो हमेशा बस चिल्लाती थी

उस दिन मेरा कमरा कुछ बिखरा सा था
और उसे तो वह काफ़ी अनचाहा सा था
संवारने वाली बात हज़ार बार बताती थी
माँ तो हमेशा बस चिल्लाती थी

मैंने एक दिन पढ़ाई से इनकार कर दिया
उसने वह भी अपने दिल पे ले लिया
ग़ुस्से में कैसे मुझे भूखा रख पाती थी
माँ तो हमेशा बस चिल्लाती थी

कभी मेरी आवाज़ पापा पे कुछ चढ़ गई
उसी वक़्त दहलाती सी एक थप्पड़ लग गई
कभी कभी कुछ पलों में बहुत डराती थी
माँ तो हमेशा बस चिल्लाती थी

झूठ बोला एक बार दोस्तों के बहाने से
मना कर दिया उसने मुझे घर आने से
कुछ बातों पे यूँ बेरहम सी हो जाती थी
माँ तो हमेशा बस चिल्लाती थी

आज...
बड़े फ़ैसलों को भी संभल के लेता हूँ
कुछ बिखर जाए तो जल्द ही संवार लेता हूँ
ख़ुद को भीड़ से आगे रख पाता हूँ
पर दुनिया से बड़े प्यार से पेश आता हूँ
हर मंजर पर सच का साथ निभाता हूँ
एक अच्छा इंसान ही तो बनना चाहता हूँ

शायद यही सब हर डाँट में सिखाती थी
माँ तो हमेशा बस चिल्लाती थी

11. Father

Remember the toy car you liked as a kid?
And it arrived one morning as a surprise?
That's when he might have had to forbid
Buying a shirt that had caught his eyes

You know how you wanted your dream shoes?
And then realised they were too expensive
But he already knew what he had to choose
Your smile over the trip with his guy crew

There was this big night-out with friends
Only that extra money seemed important
He was toiling hard, trying to meet ends
But he ensured you enjoyed every moment

When it was time to chase your dream
Only the best college was on your mind
He kept your eyes filled with that gleam
While silently he took the extra grind

Now when you may be all independent
And you are standing firmly on your feet
But if some trouble calls for an attendant
You know he will still take all the heat

One day, your kid will start those demands
And you're hit with reality of his sacrifices
Thank him today, just hold his weary hands
Life probably hasn't given him his choices

12. Miniature | Petrichor

And suddenly the clouds burst into a cry
They did not like the earth scorched and dry
The petrichor leaving all souls in a high
They begged the heavens to pierce the sky

13. Miniature | Influenced

अजीब सी हो गई है दुनिया आजकल
तिनका-तिनका ज़िंदगी जिनकी कट रही है
महलों में रहने वाले उन्हें *influence* कर रहे हैं
दिखावे के दरिया में बेख़ौफ़ बहकर
सपनों की चाह में लोग होश खो रहे हैं

14. Guftagu | Don't worry

"Don't worry, I am fine. It's just a phase."

"Well, it's a phase of your life. Why wouldn't I worry?"

15. What happened to us?

What happened to us?
How did we grow up to so much fuss?

I remember when we were little
When bodies were brittle
But minds were clean
Colours, castes, looks, disabilities
Were all unheard, unseen

And then apparently
When we are bigger, wiser as adults
And all the unheard, unseen
Has become a reason to repulse

What happened to us?
How did we grow up to so much fuss?

16. सपने

पता नहीं, सपनों को कैसे माप लेते हैं
उन्हें देखने वालों की फ़ितरत छान लेते हैं
सपने छोटे तो इंसान भी छोटा मान लेते हैं
अधूरे सपनों से क़िस्मत जान लेते हैं

पर हर एक ज़िंदगी की अलग कहानी है
किसी की सच्चाई, किसी ने ख़्वाब-सी मानी है
किसी को आसमाँ, किसी को बस रोटी कमानी है
अपने हिसाब से सबके सपनों की रवानी है

17. We keep fighting death to live

Human beings, so feeble yet so strong
Waking up every day like we belong
Journey of life, we desire to be long
A wish so pure, a thought so wrong

But we swim the tide, because we believe
Aging maturely, but for time so naïve
Wills so powerful, our minds conceive
And we keep fighting death to live

18. Miniature | हमेशा

तू यूँ ही बैठी रहे सामने
वक़्त तो ना ठहरेगा कभी
पर मेरे ख्वाब आके बस जायेंगे तेरे पास...
हमेशा!

19. Miniature | याद

याद आएगी कुछ यूँ बारिश की तरह
कि दिल और सूखा सा लगेगा

20. Miniature | Memories

Memories, like a flowing river
Flooding your heart, but drowning your eyes

Dreams, like a scented book
Dreams, like a trail of mountains
Taming your heart, but tempting your eyes

Heart and eyes, they're one, always have been
Because the eyes never forget what heart has seen

21. Guftagu | Believe

"I think I will never believe in myself."

"I do."

22. Guftagu | Sapne

"Pata nahi sapne sacchai mein kab badlenge."

"Khwahishon ko junoon banana itna aasan kahan hota hai?"

23. Heart is a mess

Ever since you made my heart your home
I felt there's so much more to my life
You filled it with love, made it your own
And I have never felt so much alive

Your joy added to it, your grief rattled some
All you do is leave my heart such a mess
But that's the beauty of it, it's never numb
You're the chaos my heart must posses

24. Freedom or Loneliness

Imagine a life with no judgements
With no bars holding you back
Doing what you want, no regrets
No one to serenade you with flak

Imagine waking up to yourself
Not a person nagging you for it
You don't need that clock for help
Make a coffee at 12 and pour it

Imagine coming back home late
And order your favourite food
No one asking to wash that plate
All the mess that you like unmoved

Imagine a life, full of freedom
Or is it a façade, a smiling face?
You want more of this life to come
But how long will you defy loneliness?

25. रुसवा

ना करना मुझसे तू शिकवा कभी
ना होना मुझसे तू रुसवा कभी

कोई पल ना सुकून से गुजरे तेरी नाराज़गी में
कोई साँस ना लगे अपनी सी
कोई नजारा ना हो जो सादगी दे
कोई बात ना लगे प्यारी सी

लगे जैसे लमहें ही निकल जाये ज़िंदगी से सभी
ना करना मुझसे तू शिकवा कभी
ना होना मुझसे तू रुसवा कभी

26. Miniature | खर्च

दूसरों के लिए जिंदगी खर्च की यूँ
खुद के लिए जीना पड़ा तो उधार सा लगा

27. Miniature | शहर

ये भीड़ ही लगती है अपनी, भले ही अपने कम हों
आगे बढ़ती ही है ज़िंदगी, भले ही सपने ग़ुम हों
ये जाना-अंजाना शहर सिखा जाता है सबक़ कई
मुस्कुरा ही लेते हैं सब, भले ही दिल गुमसुम हो

28. Guftagu | Because

"But why are you crying?"

"Because I am too happy..."

29. Think

"Babe, come here, our balcony is flooding."
He was annoyed, standing in some water
"Let's salvage what's left here floating."
Someone else's home was slaughtered

"I can't stand this unbelievable heat!"
She said in rage, turning on that AC
"Let's take kids to the shadowy street."
In scorching sun came a mother's plea

"I told you the food at this place sucked."
They fought over the choice of restaurant
"I am just trying to find what's chucked."
The hungry kid was scouring streets in hunt

"When are you getting our shower fixed?"
The teenager didn't fancy a bath otherwise
"Let's clean you with this cloth I got rinsed."
A mother was back from the leaking pipes

"I can't believe we have to drop the plan."
He cursed the broken car on the weekend
"I would have missed the shift had I not ran."
The daily wager was smiling in content

We can all cry over things being wrecked
But what we may have is actually enough
Step into others' shoes, little retrospect
Our lives, maybe, aren't even half as tough

30. पहाड़ों में

इन पहाड़ों में रफ़्तार धीमी सी है
हवाएँ अलग हैं, वादियाँ सहलाती सी हैं
लोग भले रहते हों इन छोटे मकानों में
पर हर आशियाने में एक कहानी सी है

यहाँ दिल भरे हैं, चेहरों पर मुस्कान सी है
ज़रूरतें कम, पर ज़िंदगी आबाद सी है
दिल से परोसा जाता है स्वाद थालियों में
हर निवाले में ख़ुशी की गुनगुनाहट सी है

31. Heaven and abyss

For every wrongdoing, there's a right
For every dark alley, there's a street bright
For every tear shed, there's a wide smile
For every tragic death, there's a new life

We all go through loss, for something a gain
We all bear the summers, for a pleasant rain
We all want to forget, and keep some to miss
Only on earth we have this heaven and abyss

32. Miniature | मुहाजिर

ज़िंदगी बनाने में मुहाजिर बन जाते हैं
और ज़िंदगी कहीं और छोड़ आते हैं

33. Miniature | तारीफ़

काफी शिद्दत से तारीफ़ करेंगे सब लोग
बस पहले मौत की देहलीज़ लांघनी होगी

34. Miniature | Life in a Metro

एक अजीब सी आवाज़ है इस भीड़ में
सब दिखते ख़ामोश हैं, पर शोर की जैसे झड़ी है
एक अजीब सी कश्मकश है इस हलचल में
सब दिखते गड़बड़ी में, पर ज़िंदगी कहीं अटकी पड़ी है

35. Guftagu | Fail

"I feel like I have failed too much."

"It's okay. Our love will never."

36. Guftagu | Life

"Life can be so hard sometimes."

"Yeah, because it is priceless, not easy."

37. Love?

Does love have a meaning anymore?
Or are people becoming optional?
Will they keep swiping, keep a score?
The word 'relationship' seems feeble

Their fingers were slightly gripping
But his headphones were on
I don't think he was listening
Her calls & cries seemed forlorn

Was that girl talking to herself?
Oh, she had AirPods for the call
Her mind was lost in phone's stare
Her fingers were in endless scroll

That cute couple was on a date
But that candid post was taking so long
Ah, their feeds needed to be perfect
Who cares if they actually got along

Then one day, realisation takes over
They don't feel they're the right match
Professing their followers about closure
They start swiping for a better catch

The hunt for true love will continue
But fight for it, they won't endure
Feelings fading, emotions are few
Endless possibilities, leaving them unsure

38. Choose your burden

Throughout our lives we seek comfort
Peace that our hearts and minds crave
Demons, we are not ready to confront
Dreaming of a smooth sail to the grave

But the path of life is mostly testing
The ups and downs are the only certain
And when we finally stop manifesting
We learn to fight and choose our burden

39. मुश्किलों की रवानी

ज़िंदगी में सबके मुश्किलों की रवानी है
थोड़ी हँसी, चंद आँसू... यही कहानी है
इसी सफ़र को जीकर एक बात ग़ौर से जानी है
हर क़दम पे हौसला हो, बस यही ठानी है

रूह में हिम्मत की बूँद-बूँद छानी है
घने अँधेरे में भी कभी हार न मानी है
कुछ सपने, कुछ ख़्वाहिशें ही तो पानी है
और इसलिए कभी ज़मीन आसमान से मिलानी है

ज़िंदगी की किताब किसी मिसाल-सी पढ़ानी है
फ़तेह कर लो हर दिन... भले मुश्किलों की रवानी है

40. Miniature | ख्वाहिश

ज़िंदगी से कुछ ज़्यादा ख्वाहिश नहीं है मेरी
बस तू हाथ थामे रहना अपने इश्क़ की राहों पर
और मैं रखूँगा तेरा हर एक सपना सर आँखों पर

41. Miniature | लहरें

छू कर निकल गई यूँ लहरें मुझे
जैसे तड़पाती हैं तेरी यादें मुझे
ठहर जाने का मन तो था बहुत
पर पास बुला रही थीं तेरी बातें मुझे

42. Guftagu | Long distance

"I feel connected with you, but somehow its incomplete."

"It's probably just the distance."

43. Soar High And Conquer

Your worry is pointless, time is in control
Your miseries won't ever end in a flash
Senses go numb, caged in a hapless soul
For every healed wound, there's a new scratch

The relentless life will keep being difficult
Some things on your journey won't fall your way
Just stand your ground, don't feel humbled
Be strong in there, go beyond your grey

Let it all go, the helplessness inside
Choose your path with your heart's light
Let it all go, how much you've cried
Forget the world, be true to the right

Once you decide, there's no limit to your sky
Just push through all walls, do your best
Don't ever stop growing, keep soaring high
You're born to conquer life's every quest

44. प्यार

प्यार
जाना तो सपना, महसूस करो तो जादुई
संभाला तो अपना, छोड़ा तो जुदाई
इसमें है कभी तकरार, और इसी में है लड़ाई
पर चोट लगे तो इसी ने मरहम भी लगाई

कभी है दर्द सा, तो आँख भर आई
कभी हँसाए खूब, जन्नत-सी लगे सच्चाई
लगता है यूँ कि कोई और है अब आपकी परछाई
दो जिस्मों की, एक ही धड़कन है जैसे कराई

प्यार
एक ऐसी बात जो अगर उस शख़्स को न भी बताई
फिर भी हर लम्हे में शिद्दत से है जताई

45. Separation

Separation, a sorrow
A wound that heals, but leaves its mark
A string of memories, broken, yet beautiful
A dwindling light, blowing your spark

But you find a new reason to feel joy, feel loved
You know you'll survive the tide
For every sunset, there's a new day
For every heartbreak, you'll find hope, across the divide

46. Miniature | इरादों से मुलाक़ात

रातें चाहे लंबी हों, सुबह को भला रोकेंगे कैसे?
तुम इंतज़ार को बस एक इम्तिहान समझ लेना
अनकही ख्वाहिशों को हक़ीक़त में ढालेंगे कैसे?
तुम अपने हौसलों को इरादों से मिला देना

47. Miniature | बचपन

हम ढूँढ़ते हैं कुछ चीज़ें अपने बच्चों की बेशुमारी में
और वो ढूँढ़ रहे हैं बचपन चंद चीज़ों की घरदारी में

48. Miniature | प्यार की कमी

दुनिया में प्यार की कमी नहीं है
बस ढूँढने वाले बहुत हैं, और जताने वाले कम

49. Guftagu | Tufaan

"Apni jindagi mein kaafi tufaan sa lag raha hai."

"Mujhe tairna nahi aata toh kya hua, sambhalna aata hai."

50. Guftagu | Let me forget

"Remember that night after annual function?"

"Yeah, the only thing I want to forget."

51. What's the point?

What's the point...
If we are waging wars
To dominate others
Leaving deep scars
A generation smothers

What's the point...
If races still matter
Inequality persists
Feelings shatter
People can't coexist

What's the point...
If there's still terror
Fighting faiths
Instilling horror
In damaged brains

What's the point...
If nature is choking
The endless greed
Has climate eroding
But we don't recede

What's the point...
If women still fight
For happy survival
For every right
For their revival

What's the point...
If rich rewrite laws
Rest be survivors
In world of flaws
Run by top tiers

What's the point...
If lives are digital
Adrift of feelings
We're so fickle
Seeking healings

What’s the point...
If we have forgotten to love
If we fail as human beings
The world may rise above
While humanity just bleeds

52. Chaotic bliss

Life is such a chaotic bliss.

We drown deep in love
What's not supposed to be ours
We end up in a happy tale
Imperfect partners, beautiful memoirs

Perhaps life is all about letting go
You don't turn back and ask why
Just pause in that freeing moment
Let go of the hurt, close it with goodbye.

53. हिसाब

इस ज़िंदगी में कई सपने पूरे किए
मुस्कुराकर जीते हुए हम बस चल दिए
रात की ख़ामोशी में जब भी आँख लगी
सोचा पूरी सी लग ही रही है ये ज़िंदगी

फिर भी जब यादों का पिटारा खुल जाता है
हर एक लम्हा गवाही देने आता है
मिला जो कुछ, उसी में ख़ुद को ख़ुश देखा
पर हिसाब उसी का रखा जो हासिल न हो सका

54. Miniature | तस्वीर

तुझे देखना हो तो
तू सामने हो ये ज़रूरी नहीं
आँखें बंद कर लूँ
तो दिल तेरी तस्वीर बना लेता है

55. Miniature | मंज़िल

उस पहाड़ से क्या डर,
अगर मंज़िल ही उसके पार हो
हौसलों के हर एक क़दम से
राहें बनती हज़ार हो

56. Guftagu | Ameeri

"Mujhe laga isse pehnu toh thoda amir dikhunga."

"Bewakoof, kuch fata, jhalla sa pehen."

57. रात

ये जो तारे रात को रोशन सा करें
आज कहीं खो से गए हैं
आँख नम, अरमान सो से गए हैं

बादलों ने भी घेर लिया है यूँ
जैसे अँधेरा और गहरा हो
क़ैद सा दिल धड़कना ठहरा हो

आ जाना तुम हवा की तरह
गर्दिशों को उनकी राह दिखा देना
इस रात को फिर से चाँदनी सा बना देना

58. The world breaks everyone

The world is a tough place
It breaks you at its own pace
Whether you're good, or you're worse
Whether you're blessed, or in a curse

But you've to heal, you've to mould
Those who don't, get knocked out cold
There's no shame in being broken
Let the time fill, the wound that's open

59. हज़ामत

वह भी क्या वक़्त गुज़रा है
जब हज़ामत बस एक ज़रिया होता था
दिलों को हरारत से खोल के
पंखों के नीचे
गर्मी में भी सुकून महसूस होता था

पर अब वहाँ से पंखे हट गए
AC लगवा के सलून कहलाते हैं
जगह आलिशान सी हो गई
पर बातें खो गईं
और दिल भी बस ठंडे से रह जाते हैं

60. Miniature | सवाल जवाब

जिन सवालों के जवाब पत्थरों में लिखे हों
उन सवालों को मन का बोझ बनाना बेकार है

61. Miniature | धक्का

दिल तो पहले ही फिसला हुआ है प्यार में आपके
ये रोज़-रोज़ धक्का देने की क्या ज़रूरत है?

62. Miniature | अधूरा प्यार

ना कर मुझसे प्यार इतना
जानते हैं जब अंजाम हम
ना छोड़ सकते हैं, ना भुला पाएंगे
ये कहानी ना शुरू होगी, न ख़त्म

63. Guftagu | Kaafi

"Tum jo mangoge woh tumhara!"

"Jo hai, wahi kaafi hai."

64. Guftagu | Differences

"You know me!"

"I am questioning it now."

65. Everything is fine

It was all a facade; It was all fake
He didn't realise what was at stake
How easily he could manipulate
Into thinking it's still not too late

He hid it all, master of deception
Smiling face concealing every intention
He left home, everyday, at nine
Returning nonchalantly, everything fine

But deep down, the pain had permanence
The body functioned, mind lost patience
He was buried in weight of expectations
He was suffering under his inhibitions

These men, they're so good at pretending
Holding the fort, even if the world is ending
What a bloody trick they have mastered
The crushed souls have happiness plastered

66. You

We glow like light, you're the source
We sail rough seas, you're the course
We flow like breeze, you're the air
We burn in passion, you're the flair

You make me smile, you're happiness
You make me safe, you're gentle caress
You make me better, you're my force
You make life rhythmic, you're my chorus, and my verse

67. गम और ख़ुशी

क्या है ये ज़िंदगी, कुछ ग़म न हो अगर
मुस्कुराहटों की क़ीमत वही तो तय करे
धूप सी खिली हँसी, वादियों की आए लहर
काली घटाओं से तूफ़ानी बारिश जब हो परे

दिल हर लम्हा ढूँढे ख़ुशी की एक-एक वजह
और वक़्त लिखे दास्ताँ क़िस्मतों की राहों में
आख़िरी साँस जब करने आए ज़िंदगी को रिहा
दुआ है कि बस ख़ुशियों के ही पल हमें याद रहे

68. Miniature - दूरी

कुछ खला है तुमसे दूर होके
बस यादों से तो इंसाफ़ नहीं
और ख़यालों का कोई हिसाब नहीं

69. Miniature | आवाज

उनकी आवाज़ जो दिल सहला देती थी
उसी की कमी अब दिल दहला देती है

70. Guftagu | Jatao

"Itna pyar karte ho toh baar baar jatate kyun nahi?"

"Saanson ke liye hawa ko maujudgi sabit nahi karni padti."

71. Guftagu | I do

"Will you accompany me?"

"I do..."

"I mean, yes, sure, yeah, I will."

72. Comfort zone

There's a space
You feel safe
You don't race
You just stay

It's well known
It's addictive
Comfort Zone
It's so fictive

Devoid of risks
Stunting growth
A vaccum exists
For you to float

Afraid to fail
Safe from storms
Ship won't sail
With folded arms

Breach the gates
Look outside
Magic awaits
If you don’t hide

Go be scarred
Swim the new sea
‘Cos it’s all hard
Just before it’s easy

73. मुकाम

अपने सपनों के पीछे दौड़े चले जाते हैं
और कई मुक़ाम पीछे छूट जाते हैं
जब तक हम ये जान पाते हैं
ज़िंदगी के सारे मायने बदल जाते हैं

पा लेना सपने तुम अपने हिसाब से
पर याद रखना पन्ने अपनी किताब के
पहुँच जाओगे जब अपने मुक़ाम पे
ना हों आँसू कोई, बस हँसी हो ज़ुबान पे

74. A lost place

While the world was moving at a constant pace
I felt like I was standing at a lost place
All I wanted was you beside me in that silent space
All I wanted was your smile right in front of my face

For I could cherish that moment forever
For I would not want that view to vanish, ever
For I could kiss you in that breeze and savour
As I would hold you with me and let you go never

75. Miniature | बेपनाह

कहाँ ज़िंदगी के पैमानों में ख़ुशी ढूँढ रहे हैं
दिल तो बस बेपनाह होने पर ही मुस्कुराता है

76. Miniature | एक शाम

लहरों में कुछ मनचली आवाज थी
जैसे मेरी ख़ुशी तुम्हारी हँसी की मोहताज थी
आसमान चमक रहा था रंगों से यूँ
पूरी कायनात जैसे अपने प्यार का ताज थी

77. Miniature | सब्र

सच्चा प्यार हर किसी को नहीं मिलता
क्योंकि तराशने का सब्र नहीं रहा

78. Guftagu | Fikar

"Itni fikar kyun karte ho? Bacchi nahi hu mein."

"Pyar roj bataya nahi jata, jataya jata hai."

79. Guftagu | (Mis)Understanding

"Why can't you understand me?"

"Because then I am misunderstood."

80. My valentine

There she is my lovely valentine
Lost in her endless thoughts
Forever on her, let the sun shine
Let her have the world if she wants

Her soul is selfless and kind
Covered with beauty and grace
An epitome of thoughtful mind
Woman with warmest embrace

Juggling all the lives around
Like a maestro in everything
Like a gem that I somehow found
The best of a human being

I always promise to do my best
To make her happy and smile
But I am the one who's more blessed
The way she makes it all worthwhile

As she takes care of our world
My love for her only grows with time
I got more than what I deserved
A woman, there she is, my valentine

81. साथ

तुम हो ज़िंदगी में हर पल साथ जो मेरे
हर मुश्किल हो जाए मुस्कुराहटों सी आसान
हो जाए कभी गिले-शिकवे भी साथ तेरे
बन जाए वह भी अपने प्यार की ही दास्ताँ

अगर कभी ख़फ़ा हो जाओ तुम मुझसे
मेरे पागलपन पे बस थोड़ा हँस लेना
जोड़ रखी है मेरी पूरी कहानी यूँ तुझसे
बस हर क़दम पे तुम मेरा साथ देना

82. The sea, the calm, the chaos

When the sun sets, you can hear the sea
The shore is colder, the more your feet bury
The wind is strong; The noises break free
The heart wants more, what eyes can't see

Under the steady surface, restless water
Under the soft waves, voices & chatter
Under the wetness, the sand is still hotter
The calm with chaos makes the sea better

83. Miniature | बेशुमार प्यार

इतना भी प्यार न कर मुझसे
कि किसी और ख़याल की गुंजाइश न हो
दिल को ज़ख्म जो लगे कभी
तो कहीं किसी ख़्वाब की भी कोई ख़्वाहिश न हो

84. Miniature | कभी

कभी देखा करते थे उनको जी भर के हर रोज़
अब तो आँख बंद किए बिना वह नज़ारे नहीं दिखते

85. Guftagu | Jhoot

"Jhoot kyun kaha ki tum ja rahe ho?"

"Rukne ke baad tumhari iss hansi ke liye."

86. Guftagu | Yaad

"Pata hai, abhi tumhe hi yaad kar raha tha."

"Mujhe toh yaad karne ki jarurat hi nahi padti."

87. Mirrors

You know how reflections deceive
Distortions of reality that we perceive
But there's a beauty in these mirrors
They also show us our real colours

Your eyes can't hide your own gaze
With yourself, you stand face to face
A moment of truth, taming your existence
Either free dive, or choose abstinence

८८. अधूरी सी पूरी ज़िंदगी

ये जो ज़िंदगी के छोटे-छोटे लम्हे हैं
कुछ हक़ीक़त, कुछ रंगीन सपने हैं
कहीं धूप है, कहीं छाँव और सुकून है
पाया बहुत कुछ, और पाने का भी जुनून है

दुखों के साथ कई ख़ुशियों की बारिश है
जी लेते हैं मन की, पर और जीने की गुज़ारिश है
सब कुछ है, फिर भी कुछ न कुछ बाकी है
अधूरी सी पूरी ज़िंदगी की अलग ही एक झांकी है

जैसी भी हो ये ज़िंदगी, आपके साथ ही बितानी है
ये सिर्फ़ मेरी या आपकी नहीं, हमारी पूरी कहानी है

89. Miniature | दस्तक

इन वादियों में कोहरा सा है कुछ आज
ना जाने क्या है उस पार, कुछ अनजान
ना जानने की ज़रूरत पड़ी है अब तक
और तेरे-मेरे पैर निकल पड़े वहाँ
तेरा साथ ही है मेरे हिम्मत की दस्तक

90. Miniature | अधूरे पन्ने

कभी-कभी प्यार के अधूरे पन्ने बहुत कुछ कह जाते हैं
और कभी पूरी कहानियों की किताबें कुछ ना कह पाती हैं
अधूरे एहसासों को हम ज़िंदगी का पूरा हिस्सा मानते हैं
और कभी पूरे हुए किस्सों को ज़िंदगी अधूरी कहलाती है

91. Miniature | आहट

ना जाने वह उसकी आहट थी
या था बस महकता सा वो धुआँ
महसूस हुई उसकी मौजूदगी
गवाह थी हर एक सांस, हर एक रुआँ

92. Guftagu | Alag

"Kya tum bhi wahi soch rahe ho, jo mein soch rahi hu?"

"Pata nahi, shayad apna pyaar thoda alag ho."

93. Guftagu | Dukh

"Ye dukh jindagi se khatam kab honge?"

"Shukar karo jinda ho, woh bhi jald hi jaan jaaoge."

94. End of quest

Days will pass and turn into months
Months will pass to turn into years
But you'll be the only one my heart wants
I want to share all your smiles and tears

There's so much more that I see in you
Than your pretty smile and beautiful face
The kindness, care, humility to name a few
It's all of you that makes my heart race

I must have had an envious last life
They say it rewards you in this one
Everything feels complete with you by my side
And my heart knows you're second to none

Every moment with you, I always cherish
With you, I'll always consider myself blessed
Let me be all yours till I live and perish
Let my love for you mark the end of my quest

www.ingramcontent.com/pod-product-compliance
Lightning Source LLC
Chambersburg PA
CBHW050530240926
51846CB00003B/762
* 9 7 8 9 3 7 3 1 4 7 7 6 5 *